# AN ENGLISH BALLET

Ninette de Valois

# An English Ballet

Edited by David Gayle

OBERON BOOKS

LONDON

This collection first published in 2011 by Oberon Books Ltd

521 Caledonian Road, London N7 9RH

Tel: 020 7607 3637 / Fax: 020 7607 3629

e-mail: info@oberonbooks.com

www.oberonbooks.com

Reprinted in 2011

A catalogue record for this book is available from the
British Library.

ISBN: 978-1-84943-107-1

Printed and bound by 4edge Limited, UK

# Contents

# Acknowledgements

David Gayle wishes to thank Alexander and Piers Stannus for permission to publish Madam's talk and Sir Peter Wright for permission to include Madam's Memorial Address which he gave at Westminster Abbey.

David Gayle wishes to thank Charles Shaw who suggested Madam's talk be brought to text and for his advice on the project and also thanks to Sarah Woodcock in regard to the photographs.

A portion of the royalties from the sale of the book are being generously donated to the Yorkshire Ballet Summer School.

Tues

Dear David

If you would like me to open your Seminar on _Monday Aug 4th_ — if that is the official day — please tell me some details as soon as possible — or telephone me if you want a short chat. (Telephone me a weekend at anytime)

Madam

# *Foreword*

I was thrilled when Ninette de Valois accepted my invitation to give a talk at the Yorkshire Ballet Seminars at Ilkley College in August 1981 during the 50th Anniversary celebrations of The Royal Ballet. This was a very busy year for her and she was now eighty-three.

Before the talk, I collected her at the hotel to take her with Alicia Markova and Barbara Fewster to Ilkley College in a horse-drawn carriage. On seeing the carriage, she laughed and said, 'she hadn't been in one of these since she was a little girl growing up in Ireland.' When we arrived at the college, she gave this compelling talk for about an hour without notes.

*David Gayle MBE*

'Madam your carriage awaits!'
On route to Ilkley College, 2nd August 1981.
Dame Ninette de Valois, Dame Alicia Markova,
David Gayle, Barbara Fewster.
*Photograph: courtesy of the author*

# 1. De Valois' Address to the Yorkshire Ballet Seminars

I have been asked to talk to you first of all about the fifty years of The Royal Ballet's life. Well, fifty years you know for a classical tradition in a country is a very short one. In fifty years we've not only had to build up an English school but an English company, English dancers and above all English choreography and also from those things, of course, there springs what is now known as the English style. Well, like all things that get a title they can get very confusing.

I am told what the English style is now all over the world and, believe it or not, I don't think I know any longer what it is, as many people have slightly different views. Style is something to do with character, style is something to do with the personalities that spring from the character of the country, style has a great deal to do with its national dances and people dance national dances through themselves. They are the invention of the native country and so we go back to look at those things very carefully to realise what really our style springs from.

I don't think our national dances among the classical ballet teachers in the country are taken anything like seriously enough. I don't think they know to what depth we owe all these steps and when I say national dances I would spread it and say not just England, Ireland, Scotland and Wales – I would say the whole of Western Europe. I don't think they quite know how much we owe to the national dances of all these countries for our fundamental technique. Our position is exactly the same as music. We know how airs and tunes and melodies have been lifted and turned into in the past really very complicated symphonies. We know this, we know how this has inspired operas and the same thing happens in the ballet world and this is something I would like the teachers and the students of today to realise.

When we introduced national dances to our School, must be now about twenty five years ago, there was real consternation among the students. They thought it was a dreadful idea. Now, of course, it is one of the highlights of their work and gradually, as I hoped, they are being sent abroad to show how these dances can be danced by trained dancers. Other countries have been very acute about seeing that their national dancers that they send away were trained dancers and knew what they were doing. We were much more narrow and thought the fatter the gentleman was, the more quaint it was and the more like the dance and it is not true. I can't watch in the past fifty years, or rather before that, some of the national dances done in this country by people who were either too old to do it or never bothered to learn them properly because everyone thought it was absolutely wonderful, and that it shouldn't be done in any other way and, whatever happens, they must never point their toes, etc.

You know that is really all nonsense when you see what Eastern Europe has done to itself with the development of their national dances, and I want to see ours developed like this. They are creeping into some of our ballets. You have all seen *la Fille mal gardée* and seen what Sir Frederick Ashton has done in some of the dances in that. It's important to get this very thing they call style and character and it was a triumph for us last year that The Royal Ballet Lower School boys and girls in their national dances were sent to Israel to represent English folk dancing, and they had a very good success because it was the first time they had seen trained dancers do our dances and they suddenly realised how beautiful it could be and the huge technical demand in some of them. It is also very good for the rhythm for everything. Now here ends my lecture on the importance of the national dance. It is important. Don't overlook it and try and make the children realise it.

There is another very close affinity to the classical world in school and that is Dalcroze Eurhythmics. For the national dance you go to our national heritage to bring it up to make classicism. Classicism springs from the roots of the country whatever form of classicism it is – whether it is music or plays or, as I said, dancing. The other thing is the music side and I still think that the greatest affinity we have in the country to become a part of the classical dancers' training and in school where they think they are going to learn ballet – Dalcroze Eurhythmics. Here the child is taught from the beginning of time to listen – to listen to the music, to dance with the music, understand what it is all about. This again is something that can be grossly and completely overlooked in classical ballet as taught all over the country. Not enough importance is given to the child's understanding of what she must know she is dancing to. She must interpret her music. Also, the scientific side of the music structure for the dancer is so beautifully given for, as I say, the classical dancer through Eurhythmics. There is body movement in it which is important and there is knowledge built up of music in relation to the choreographer's work later on.

Choreography; any choreographer in my opinion, should study Eurhythmics when he is young. He will find the value of it when he is older. I was lucky enough to have about three years of it when I was very young and time and time again as I got older I had forgotten nearly everything about it, I'm afraid, because I wasn't too well taught, but it is beautifully taught now and I still found myself determined to do it when it came to choreography – to understand the combination of rhythm and time signatures whenever I was creating.

So remember classicism springs from the roots of all the arts. Don't let's just talk about ballet as if it was something just by itself there. It has these great roots behind it which all young dancers whatever their future is going to be – a dancer, a teacher, a choreographer – should follow faithfully and learn about when they are very young. It is up to the schools, the state schools and such like places to see this is encouraged. I hope one day the classical ballet, pure classicism, will have the same role in the schools as music has today. We have quite a long way to go to get this problem straightened out, but straightened out it must be.

You can't do everything you know in fifty years. You can get things started and I do promise you one thing which is very interesting. As the ballet grows through time in any country or any continent you will never find all three parts of it are in perfect unity except perhaps at the very beginning or when you are forming a new company. I am talking about the art of composition, choreography and the art of pure dance – the ballerinas and artists and pedagogy, the teaching. Now when you start, it is a great effort to make these three things come together and be developed together. Always as time goes on, one predominates over the other and you have to check up and pull up on the thing that has got into the arrear. It is understandable that the country in its first roots (as we were fifty years ago) starting off on forming a big classical school, a traditional classicism, that the things that really came first didn't lead to deep roots. In choreography which was creative work there were plenty of frustrated choreographers knocking about the world when we started, particularly in England. I was one of them, and there were plenty of dancers who were going elsewhere to dance and very successfully. Many a fine dancer was made by a foreign company. We have Diaghilev's very last choice with us today, Alicia Markova who was a little girl of fourteen and to make her way had to join the Diaghilev Company. I am giving you examples of people who had to go elsewhere so that wasn't so difficult for us when we started, actual dancing.

What is difficult, and is still behind both the choreography and the dancers is the teaching in the country. We haven't yet established our classical roots as strongly as I hope to see it established in the next fifty years. I shan't be here, of course, to see it but that is the great thing. You've got to concentrate on the immediate future, to really make up our minds what will represent the English classical school and we can only do this thing by taking from everybody else steadily or through time for another hundred years the great schools of the world – the Danish school, the French school, the Italian school and now the Russian school. We have to watch this and not drop our research in this direction. We have to find out exactly what style of anybody is right for the English physique and its development. What weaknesses in it are best strengthened by certain things from certain countries. Then we shall have a real English school, but that comes last.

We have gone quite a distance in the time. Great work has been done we know by such societies as The Royal Academy of Dancing, the Imperial Society of Dancing, the Cecchetti Society. They have all done their stint, and a very good one, but from the purely professional view we have got to look further afield and see what still has got to be added to this problem. You see you have to realise we mustn't lose the highlights of our style. We are by nature quick dancers – speedy, light – we are by nature more lyrical than dramatic, we are by nature strong demi-character dancers. We have a strong sense of acting, of characterisation – stronger than many of the other countries. Now we mustn't lose those highlights and it is bound to reflect to a certain extent in our pedagogy. We have got to think of this and not lose it, not steal too much from some other particular style which isn't really for us.

I will try to explain what I mean to you a little more academically. As I say, the root of all classicism is from the root of the country's own arts, natural arts, so we have to look to the whole of Europe and look at their folk dancing – from Spain, from France, the Basque dancers, from Scotland, from England, from Ireland, from everywhere to watch what is our highlight and it is this incredible speed, wonderful footwork. The *entrechat* is still beaten by the Basque dancers, in fact it was taken from the Basque dancers into the classical school. When I go to the Folk Dance Society and watch, I can see all our basic technical steps. This is something I think a lot, if I may say so quite firmly, our education authorities don't quite realise how basic we are. It is not artificial the ballet, it is very basic of what goes on in the country. Artificiality is only a means of bringing it up to great point of development in the theatre but its roots are very simple and very thorough. Don't imagine it is artificial, there is nothing artificial about it.

Now what I want you to realise which is so interesting – we know of this precision, the speed, this lightness of movement, this neatness and this very thing that the Americans so adore and call the English style, real style. Well, I have pointed all the countries to you that have basically given us all this work. Now I want you to see how it changes. Therefore, when we come to classicism, you mustn't imagine you have got to copy the classicism of another country because it's wonderful, because it's popular! They copy yours in the long run so be careful! I am alluding to Russia. As you move from Western Europe to Eastern Europe there is an incredible change in the folk dancing. We dance from the waist down. They dance more from the waist up. As you get further East, more and more body movement comes into it, less and less footwork. Now Eastern Europe had to take its classicism originally – I am talking about behind the whole of the Iron Curtain – they had to take their classicism from Western Europe. French ballet masters, Italian ballet masters, Danish ballet masters all went to Russia to do work for them but, because of their own basic plastic quality in all their own national dances, as it were, because of that, this has crept into their pure classical style and good luck to it. It is right. We all know and admire and adore the pure Russian classical dancer but do realise that not all of it is for us; for us to try and lavishly copy would be a very great mistake and we should lose our identity entirely, just as they would lose theirs if they hadn't allowed the influence of their own wonderful folk dances, marvellous dances as we all know, creep up and colour the Western European classical school.

You will always find that your own choreographers, your own forward theatrical productions spring from your own roots; don't kill it off because it is loved outside your own country. You may get bored with it but other people are not bored with it. I have just come back from New York and I know they are not. They think it wildly exciting and lovely to see and this attitude of preservation of what is ours is a part of our education authorities to realise – they must look to this and not forget it in their search for what they think are easier movement and easier learning for their children. There is nothing more horrible than classicism badly taught. Because it is so good! The better taught it has to be, the more profound its foundations and everything, the better the teaching has got to be. So look out!

I return to the question of the fifty years. As you know, we started off in a very small way at the theatre built by that very marvellous woman Lilian Baylis who, like me, believed in bricks and mortar before anything and she always said that, when she had the Sadler's Wells Theatre built, she would put my school into it and form an English ballet. So we did have this wonderful group to start with and we had alongside us a drama company and an opera company and so the classicism of our ballet company was started in the most perfect way, I think, in the same way as the Paris Opera was started, although it was on a very small scale, the same way the Italian school, Danish school and the Russian school were started – alongside the drama and the Opera and they were inseparable.

We made our biggest progress in the war at the time when the first thing the Home Office did was to say every theatre had to close down. There was no time for any sort of entertainment. War was war and that was the end of it, but it wasn't. They soon found that the one thing people in this country needed during that terrible period was the theatre and I cannot tell you how the theatre grew in the war. Sensibly they threw their theatres open to drama, to opera, and to ballet and, if it hadn't been for the work done by the Sadler's Wells and the Old Vic before the war, we would have been very poorly served because they were the big things that survived right through the war. Really!

It was much more difficult to run individual plays and companies. It was the establishment split up that survived the war and educated an enormous public who up to then had never gone into a theatre at all. The ballet played the biggest part because it was the newest thing and it was new to so many people that saw us. We built our public, real public, up during the war years. It was a fantastic experience. I remember when we were sent at the end of the war to Brussels and Paris to entertain the troops, our own troops, going there for the first time. I shall remember the extraordinary sensation. We were sent only to dance for the troops. The war when we got to Brussels was still going on – I think about fifty miles outside the capital – and the troops were coming into Brussels on 48-hour leave. They had nothing to do but go to the theatre and, when we were there, they had nothing to do but go to the ballet – long khaki queues outside the Garrison Theatre. We built up a great public of people who had never been inside the theatre to see a ballet before. I always remember hearing one man come out, war weary old boy he was, he had sat through a performance of *The Rake's Progress* and coming out of it he said 'I never knew a ballet could be about anything.'

Then we had the excitement of going to Paris where we made our first big contact with America because the theatre they put us in was closed to everyone but the American troops. Americans didn't know anything about our company, which was called in those days the Sadler's Wells Ballet, and they were hustled into this place for entertainment and we built up a very big American public. So many of them remembered us and many came to see us years later when we opened in New York. I also remember when we went to the Paris Opera to meet the Paris Opera dancers, a magnificent school, the first school in Europe. The root of all our classicism is the French school and we must never forget it. We still use their language all over the world for our technical terms. We went to meet the Paris dancers who had struggled through the war, cut off from everything and everybody. They were dying to come and see us because they hadn't seen anything but they weren't allowed to because it was forbidden. Nobody but the troops could come. We couldn't get the Paris Opera dancers into our theatre to see us. I may as well tell you that the dress uniform were E.N.S.A. uniforms then, they were just officer's uniforms – khaki for both the men and the girls worn by all the entertainers who were part of the army when we went on these expeditions. There was in Paris at that time a drama company and I think a concert party – all the E.N.S.A. performers were in one big hotel together. Well, we couldn't get the Paris Opera in so I had to give it up in the end.

I remember going in front of house one night. It was full of American troops and I suddenly saw an enormous amount of E.N.S.A. people, boys and girls, in uniform. I thought 'I wonder what has happened – have they sent a new drama company out of England, have they sent some concert group or what have they sent?' I had another look at them all and I got a little suspicious. So I went backstage to this enormous dressing room the company were in and, when I went in, everyone was frightfully busy making up – extra busy – so I looked around the room and there wasn't a single English E.N.S.A. uniform hanging up on the wall and then I knew how the Paris Opera Ballet had got in to see us.

So that was a very exciting and wonderful tour and, as I say, we built up an American public. Our next excitement was to open the Royal Opera House at Covent Garden. The Royal Opera House had only been open for three months out of the year before the war and closed for the rest of the time. We opened it and the idea was that it should be permanently opened on a subsidy now for opera and ballet for the future. Two arts came together again to help each other. We had to do it, though, alone for about eight months because the opera company wasn't ready to come in.

It was a strange coincidence for me that I came into the Opera House at Covent Garden in 1946 with an English ballet company, and in 1919 when the First War finished and they opened the Opera House again after a four year closure for an opera season only for three months in the summer – I happened to go in as a prima ballerina for that opera season. So I went in after the

First World War as a young dancer and I went in after the Second World War as a head of an English ballet company. Strange coincidence that it took two wars to do that!

You know our history. We had our highlights. One of the most exciting, of course, was when we went to open in New York in 1949. New York really made us internationally. We were taken there for the first time to the old Metropolitan Opera House and that is a night I shall never forget. They had heard a great deal about us, we had a pretty big name in Europe by then and, of course, our Covent Garden season with the Opera Company was nine months out of the year but we were absolutely new to a real American public and it was an awful night, that opening night, wondering what was going to happen. It was a night we shall never forget, the generosity of the spirit with which they greeted us and kept up year after year. It was one of the most touching things I can recollect.

I do remember that for me it was nostalgic to go back this last summer. I went back with The Royal Ballet to celebrate their 50th Anniversary and the American public is quite extraordinary about us. They really do accept us as a sister art of theirs entirely. I hadn't been to New York for about twenty-five years except for two days three years ago, I think it is. There were almost as many people stopping me around the Metropolitan Opera House in the mornings when I went there for rehearsals as there are round Covent Garden today. They remember you, coming up to me by the dozen. It was very, very touching, really like being in London. I have never known such an extraordinary experience. They just adore the English ballet over there and it made me very happy the way we were able to welcome the American Ballet when they came over here two years ago with the Balanchine Company when it came to the Royal Opera House. Balanchine has in America formed very much an American school, classical ballet for them, that suits them down to the ground, suits their line and their style. The more prolonged lethargic line of the Russian school does suit the American dancer far better than our quick work would, if I may say so, and that is why they find us refreshingly new and different and they come over here and we find them refreshingly new and different, but as long as we want it like that, it's good. That's the way to progress, not deciding that we have got to drop the whole thing altogether and become completely like something else. We have as big a success in the States as any of the American companies but they have gone their own way, which is good. I appreciate the fact that we have learnt enough through our own

School in England for anyone over here to appreciate their style.

There may be one or two things the critics are absolutely right to say when visiting companies come here but this is just their own personal view and which they are entitled to. They go night after night, they must know what they really like and they have to say so but the critics have got to keep a slightly broader line over certain things and not decide that, because they love the schooling of another country, we must have it exactly like that. That's not possible. We have got to be choosing the dancers, looking for physiques of our own people and understanding the psychology of the English mentality and everything. So read your criticisms, they are good for us to read and don't be too waylaid by either the praise or the blame, criticism is the thing you have got to take quietly in your stride.

The other side, of course, we have to think of is the career. A lot of people forget that it is just like the opera or the drama world where it is not one career. That is an awful idea – like a gymnast or a tennis player's future career – but the wide career a dancer has within his own hemisphere is marvellous. An actual dancer's career does end somewhere about forty-two. You are lucky if you go on till then but people forget what goes into making up a school and a company. They forget you have got to have ballet masters which are the same as a chorus master. You have got to have répétiteurs, people who can rehearse special solo roles, the same as the répétiteur in the opera world. You have got to have teachers. You have got to have choreologists (people who write down difficult notation), and we have a very brilliant English notation now called Benesh which is taught or rather taken in by every opera house in Europe and in the States. It is the notation for the theatre, actually the best, and has a big career ahead of it in that direction. You have got to find people who can do that and then above all you have got to find the choreographer.

Now all these people exist in embryo in every dancer. Every dancer has one of these other things in them and it is up to teachers and it is up to the staff in the company afterwards – and very much up to the artists themselves – to not go on dancing but find which branch in dancing they would be able to develop themselves later on. That is why earlier in this talk I was talking to you about the development of the sidelines in the education of a child, its national dancing, its music, its eurhythmics, its notation, all these things because you will suddenly find a girl or a boy shows enormous promise in school. Even in the junior school of The Royal Ballet School we can pick out budding people who in the future will be choreologists or who will be good teachers, choreographers and so on and it is up to a company to encourage this right through their careers to prepare them for the second half of their career, and so many of them in the end, particularly if they haven't got to the top, have found in the second half they have got to the top in one of those other branches. But, it is not always the great dancer that makes the great teacher, although to be a great teacher – this is a very Irish remark – you have probably have had to have been a very good dancer. But, if you watch the progress of the artist, you will see some highlight in them which has nothing to do with just the dancing and please encourage them, even as children in schools, please encourage this side because that may be their future career entirely and absolutely.

I will tell you a funny little story about myself just to show you how you can see things in a very strange way in a child. When I was about eleven, I was dancing in an ordinary small school somewhere, not a professional school. I was one of a family of four, the second of the family not the eldest, and I discovered a little folk play for children about six or seven pages long with about eight characters in it and I realised that with our friends we could put this on. We had a very big drawing room in one of those old fashioned houses in London. We could put this play on for a charity performance and make all the grown-ups come and pay. So I set to and I cast it. I cast the whole thing and I put all my friends and my family I thought were right for the roles. Then I took it to my governess and I said 'Look at this, this is what we are going to do.' She said 'Yes dear, it is very nice but you haven't given yourself a role.' I said, 'No, I think someone has got to look after the play.' Now, how did I know anything? It was some strange instinct in me, I suddenly saw the whole thing with no one in control, in other words I produced it. I knew someone had to produce it. From the very beginning this is what I really wanted to do. I didn't want to be in it. Not with this other bigger job! So you just watch the children. We have great fun at White Lodge watching them when some of the children do the choreographic things.

There is a lovely story of a small boy once at White Lodge who was a budding choreographer, not extremely talented but there was a little flair showing in him that he rehearsed wonderfully. He was only about eleven. I remember the story of him collecting his dancers like a sergeant-major because he wanted to go and rehearse at once and one small girl said, 'But I want to have my tea.' He said, 'You don't want any tea, you are coming to rehearse, you don't want any tea, you are too fat anyway.' That is a budding ballet master. He wasn't going to stand any nonsense from anyone.

It is fascinating, do encourage them – not just think you've got to get on the end of your toes and isn't that lovely, there I am, I am going to be a Margot Fonteyn. There is much more to it than that. So many ways. Some of these children even turn from dancing to the music side – they are so musical, so much more talented musically than their dancing and so we encourage them to go in that direction. We had quite a talented boy who finished up in the Youth Orchestra as he played the violin better than he danced – quite simple but it was through the dancing he found the right profession.

Now I have talked for a solid hour and I think that is enough. Thank you very much for listening so beautifully.

Marguerite Porter in the Graduate Class at The Royal Ballet School
in 1965 being taught by Madam
*Photograph by Lord Snowdon, Camera Press London*

Dame Ninette de Valois, OM CH DBE and David Gayle MBE
at the opening of the first residential Yorkshire Ballet Seminars
at Ilkley College in August 1975
*Photograph: courtesy of the author*

## 2. *Madam and the Yorkshire Ballet Seminars*

*(now known as Yorkshire Ballet Summer School)*

By David Gayle

It is hard to believe it is thirty years since Madam gave this talk to the Yorkshire Ballet Seminars. De Valois' inspirational thoughts, extraordinary foresight and her memories in this talk are of great importance to everyone interested in the dance world and especially young ballet students of today and their teachers.

When I was preparing my first residential Yorkshire Ballet Seminar, which was to take place at Ilkley College, in August 1975, I wrote to Dame Ninette asking her if she would teach at the Seminar. Madam thought her teaching days were almost over, but she would be happy to open it. She didn't want a fee and she wanted to stay in a cheap hotel. Naturally, I didn't place her in a cheap hotel. I arranged for her to stay in the delightful Troutbeck Hotel, on the edge of Ilkley Moor. The day before the opening, Madam travelled from London to Yorkshire on the train with Dame Alicia Markova, and in the evening, the three of us had dinner together in the hotel discussing the future of the seminars.

The next day Madam gave a splendid opening address and then Dame Alicia Markova taught the first Master Class. Other teachers for this first residential seminar included Lynn Seymour, Wayne Sleep, Peter Clegg and Walter Trevor. Lesley Collier gave a demonstration introduced by Nicholas Dromgoole and Lynn Seymour gave a demonstration with Clement Crisp. This was the first residential ballet seminar of its kind to be held in Britain and it got off to a flying start.

Prior to this, I held non-residential courses in a church hall in Ilkley. I taught the classes in the beginning and then I invited Maryon Lane from the Royal Ballet School to teach followed by Brenda Last and Julia Farron. Two promising young students attending at the time were David Bintley and Iain Webb. David and Iain were both from Yorkshire, as were most of the students at the time. When the residential seminars began at Ilkley College the students came from all over the country and abroad.

Over the years, Madam became very involved in the Seminars and one of the highlights of the Seminar was her talk with Dame Alicia Markova going back to their first meeting in 1925, days with the Diaghilev Company and the beginnings of the Vic-Wells Ballet.

It was Madam's suggestion I start a teachers' course at the Seminar. Madam said she would take charge of the first one and she suggested I invite Julia Farron to assist her. Unfortunately, Madam couldn't come, due to unforeseen circumstances, and Julia Farron stood in her place. Madam had said to me – it was very good I was helping the students in that part of the country but she insisted I also give help to the teachers. I told her the teachers were able to watch all the classes but she thought, in addition to this, it was a good idea to have them on their own without their pupils. Those teachers attending the course, under the expert guidance of Julia Farron, enjoyed the experience and learnt a great deal. The following year Madam was able to come and help the teachers. How fortunate for all those present.

The main reason I set up the Seminar, in the first place, was to bring the very best people of our profession and from the theatre to teach the students and also, most importantly, to look for and nurture the talent. I wanted to offer top class tuition at low cost, and thanks to the generous support of kind sponsors I was able to do this and give many scholarships. I established an annual boy's scholarship in the name of David Blair, the distinguished Royal Ballet Principal dancer. David, a fellow Yorkshireman, was coming to teach at the Seminars, but sadly died a few days before at the age of 43. The first winner of the scholarship was Kevin O'Hare, chosen by Brenda Last. Others who later benefited from this award included Thomas Whitehead and David Pickering, currently in the Royal Ballet and Robert Parker and Iain Mackay, now in the Birmingham Royal Ballet. Also the dancer/actor William Kemp. Girl's scholarships were also given, chosen from the previous seminar. Two of the winners of the Markova Scholarship were Samara Downs, now in the Birmingham Royal Ballet, and Elizabeth Harrod, who is in the Royal Ballet. Samara, who came every year to the Seminar for about eight years, later said how much she had benefited from all the teachers, especially Kevin Haigen, ballet master of the Hamburg Ballet.

There were, of course, many talented students who came to the Seminars – Susan Pond, Andrea Tredinnick, Errol Pickford, Vanessa Palmer, Paul Liburd, Kenneth Tharp, William Trevitt, Russell Maliphant, Matthew Dibble and Paul Lewis to name but a few.

In 1965, Madam made a special arrangement for me to be the first male student to study on her newly formed Craftsman's Course at The Royal Ballet School – which later became known as the Teachers' Course. Madam formed this course really to help students with an interest in teaching and at the very beginning the course was for girls. I was delighted when Madam made the arrangement for me to be on it as I had always been interested in the teaching side. I was only on the course for a term and a half and Sir Frederick Ashton, the Director of The Royal Ballet, wanted me to join the Company. I went to Madam for her advice. I said I was enjoying the Craftsman's Course enormously and I had been approached by Sir Frederick to join the Company. What would she advise? Madam said, 'You must join the Company, learn more about this profession, and you can teach later.' Within a moment, Madam went into Sir Frederick's office and came out a couple of minutes later, saying 'It is all organised, you are in the Company.'

After a short period, Madam handed the Teachers' Course to Valerie Adams to direct, which she did for many years very successfully. Some years later, when I was organising the first Royal Ballet Summer Schools at White Lodge, the Junior School of The Royal Ballet, Valerie asked me to collect Madam by car, at her home in Barnes, and bring her to The Royal Ballet School for the annual student teachers' diploma day, where Madam handed out diplomas. It was a big responsibility for me to drive this great lady through London traffic and I was always slightly nervous. I need not have been, as she always put me at ease.

In the summer of 1994, when Madam was 96 she came, on a very hot evening, to my party at the Accademia Italiana, in Knightsbridge, to celebrate 21 years of the Yorkshire Ballet Seminars. There were many wonderful artists at the party who had been involved with the Seminar including Dame Alicia Markova, Dame Beryl Grey, Irina Baronova, Pamela May, Leslie Edwards, Barbara Fewster, Wayne Sleep and Pandit Ram Gopal. Also present was Audrey Burton, one of my devoted sponsors. Unfortunately, my former dancing teacher Margaret Jaffe, who helped me so much in my early training and arranged for my audition at The Royal Ballet School was unable to come. I was very touched Madam came to the party, especially at her age, but she was determined to be there and it meant a great deal to me. I was always very grateful for her support of the Seminars and indeed for all the support from the many world-famous dancers and teachers who took part.

The Yorkshire Ballet Summer School, which is now held at York St. John University, will soon be approaching its 40th anniversary. Marguerite Porter, who was Madam's protégé in the Graduate Class at The Royal Ballet School, and then a Principal dancer of The Royal Ballet, has been director of the Summer School since 2005. Marguerite, who taught at the Seminars for many years, is doing a splendid job, introducing new innovations and also very much following the traditions that I aspired to. I think Madam would have been very pleased.

7 June 1994

My dear David,

        I was very touched to receive your
flowers.  I have always been very proud of
the way you have built up the Yorkshire
Ballet Seminar so many years ago.
My hearty congratulations - you really have
achieved something for the English ballet
scene.

        I look forward to seeing you on the 24th.

                With love,

                Madam

Dame Alicia Markova and Michael O'Hare
at the first residential Yorkshire Ballet Seminars
*Photograph: courtesy of the author*

As a young man I spent two summers attending the
Yorkshire Ballet Seminars, and was lucky enough to
be taught by some of the brightest stars of the Ballets
Russes: Dame Alicia Markova, Alexandra Danilova and
Irina Baronova, as well as the remarkable Bournonville
teacher Hans Brenaa, and the unforgettable Leslie
Edwards. I was very conscious of the knowledge that
was being passed on to me by these living legends.

Kenneth Tharp, OBE, Chief Executive of The Place
*Source: Dancing Times, May 2010*

Ninette de Valois, Aged 17

The following extract is from *Gala Peformance: A Record of The Sadler's Wells Ballet Over Twenty-Five Years* with kind permission from Harper Collins and Mr Alexander Stannus. The article was written by Ninette de Valois in 1955 expressing her views on ballet at that time. Some of the things she was looking for have, of course, transpired.

\* \* \*

## Some Problems of Ballet Today

by Ninette de Valois

I am often asked what, in my opinion, is the most significant aspect of our ballet today, and my answer is the acceptance of this art as a vital part of our contemporary theatre. This recognition does not end with our position as a separate branch of cultural entertainment, for it brings in its wake a further influence, namely, the effect of the ballet on the production of much of the contemporary opera and classical drama.

We know that the classical ballet was born 300 years ago with the contemporary modern theatre, and played its part alongside the opera and drama until a short period of inglorious decline towards the end of the last century reduced the importance of its position. Until then, as it now succeeds in doing again, it infused into the theatre in general those aspects of the dance that form an integral part of many theatrical presentations.

Mime, period movement, poise and carriage are the gifts of the ballet to actor and singer, and the understanding of mass movement and of grouping is our contribution to the technique of the producer. Indeed, the work of the early ballet masters of the French Court stretched far beyond their groups of professional dancers. The correspondence between David Garrick and Noverre makes fascinating reading, for it shows the great actor in a generous mood, bestowing his patronage on the famous ballet master, and expressing his undoubted belief in the influence of Noverre on the theatre.

But it must be admitted that there was a moment during the last decade in England when the influence of the ballet on the production of classical drama became somewhat exaggerated. I have frequently stated how depressing it is to see a 'bad ballet' instead of a good dramatic production, and Sir John Gielgud raised his voice some months ago in a firmly expressed opinion on the present-day tendency of 'balletic' production of classical plays. But this phase is now under control and our influence, consequently, has a more dignified part to play.

The rise of the classical ballet of late, and the demand for full-length classical works, show a healthy reaction on the part of both the general and the specialized audience. Herein lie our beginnings, and our future tradition will evolve from such contacts none the worse for such exacting task-masters. Sadler's Wells, the largest subsidized ballet in England, is not yet a quarter of a century old. Consider the importance of its tie with its classical tradition, and the effect on the mental discipline and visual discrimination of today's young audience and artist, and realize its influence on the choreographer of tomorrow.

I must now try to answer a question that is asked with unfailing regularity – 'What do I feel about modern ballet?' 'What is its position in relation to the classical?' 'Is it a challenge?' Firstly, I bother myself little about my feelings or those of my contemporaries. Secondly, its 'position in relation to' is a journalistic cliché, endeavouring economically and aesthetically to answer a question that is neither definable nor founded on common reasoning. Thirdly, creative work is not necessarily an aggressive 'challenge'. It should be a virile natural force introducing new forms in each succeeding generation.

Today, as yesterday, in all fields of creative work we are expressing our contemporary thoughts, ideals and beliefs. This is all in order and all to the good, and let us not be puzzled or pained when we realize that we cannot see the wood for the trees. The choreographer, dramatist or musician of any country is either self-consciously of his age or a 'time-traveller'. But all forms of creative work of any epoch are dominated by their artists' sense of destruction or construction; in other words, we express through channels of revolution or evolution, and in many cases – in particular in that type of work coyly labelled 'provocative' – we are too close to our own times to judge what is on the ascent or descent with any true clarity of thought.

It is only a man of unusual vision who can discern with unfailing surety between these two fundamentals in relation to all creative work happening in his time. The average man is rooted within the midst of the ensuing turmoil. Was it not the same one hundred years ago? How few of the ballets of the great Petipa have survived the passage of time? But it matters little; for the part speaks for the whole, and we are now content to see only the best ballets of the great masters of the past as a means of obtaining a sense of proportion towards their particular period. The same may be said for the first twenty-five years of the modern classical ballet. The surviving repertoire of the Diaghilev era is a modest one, taking into account the fact that the Company was in existence for twenty years.

All modern tendencies in the ballets of Europe and America are today in a hesitant mood, and they, of course, consist of good, bad and indifferent works.

That we may frequently misjudge or misunderstand each other is a good sign; it may well mean that we are unconsciously showing certain national characteristics, without which the art of a country becomes devitalized.

But for a moment I would speak personally of today's short contemporary ballet, and I would speak of it in general. It is packed with involved movement and tortured symbolism, and I do not think that we need wait any longer to realize that the second half of this century should deal with something more than our present 'Ballet Digest'. We are in danger of choking ourselves with this condensed technical approach. Themes beg for development, movement needs more light and shade, more bridging should be permitted from one dance movement to another, and a sharp dividing line accepted and adhered to between mere acrobatics and the portrayal of lineal elegance.

The ballet's new architectural form could now be given a more gracious expansion for the theatre is tired of the brief comment, and it awaits a leisurely, well-constructed statement. I suggest that the journalistic stage of modern ballet has had its day; it is time for the flowering of its true literature. So let us suppose that we have reached an important cross-road, where we will pause to recognize certain broad principles. The technique of today needs discipline and pruning, if it is to fulfil the demand now prevailing for full-length modern works. This must become, in our future plans, the joint responsibility of librettist, composer and choreographer. Modern artists of the dance have stated their case to the world for nearly half a century in short, sharp sentences; let them now endeavour to show us that their brief comments can end in a philosophy that is now constructive, let them show that they recognize construction as of more importance than that half-way house to destruction – provocation for the sake of being provocative.

But it is firstly the problem of music, for sound can evoke a mood and stress a statement, with more speed and impact than visual movement. Music 'adapted' to ballet is an increasing menace; a return to the specially composed score is of primary importance, for here lies the true collaboration. When the choreographer, librettist and composer work together from the first on a new ballet composition they establish, at the outset, the intention to unify. It is that rarity, complete unity, that is both the simple and the complex answer to a successful work; failure is often and again not a matter of the 'choreography' or of the 'music' but an original oversight as to the relative values concerning the part with the whole. In the same way this 'unity' should underline the policy of a Company and the principles of its training school.

Our next effort lies in theatrical presentation, for once again choreography must accept the discipline and demands of the theatre. It must come to terms with the painter and his position in the theatre. We live in constant danger of losing all contact with those high standards set by Diaghilev concerning the perfect collaboration of choreography with décor and costume. In many countries Companies show equality of Terpsichorean material, but when it comes to the other Muses concerned, there are many and varied states of chaos.

Both in Europe and America the world is well served with established choreographers and promising members of the younger school. Dancers are numerous, and they are gifted, varied and exceedingly versatile. What we need is a spring-clean in the form of a general survey; we might tolerate a slogan. Dare I suggest 'Production Where Art Thou?'

Sir Peter Wright, CBE DMUS
*Photograph © Bill Cooper*

# Madam's Memorial Address

*Westminster Abbey, 28th September 2001*

By Sir Peter Wright CBE
Director Laureate, Birmingham Royal Ballet

Today we are celebrating the life of Dame Ninette de Valois, or 'Madam' as she was always called, one of the most brilliant women of the 20th century whose influence on the world of dance will certainly be felt and appreciated for many centuries to come. She was a born leader, and, although at times she could be contradictory, impatient and even ruthless in her pursuit of the establishment of a great National Ballet organisation, she was a very caring and compassionate human being and valued more than anything the love and trust of her husband, her family, her friends and her many disciples. She may have been hard on them at times, but she always held them very close to her heart.

I first met Madam in 1942 when the war was at its height and her company, the then Sadler's Wells Ballet, was appearing at the New Theatre (now the Albery) as the Sadler's Wells Theatre had been bombed. The very young Margot Fonteyn and the dynamic Robert Helpmann were the stars, surrounded by such greats as Pamela May, Beryl Grey, Moira Shearer, June Brae, Celia Franca, Julia Farron and Pauline Clayden… The men were in short supply as most of them had been called up. I was desperate to be a dancer, already seventeen, and went to see her there with my father. We had to wait in a pokey little office for two hours, and when she finally whirled in, full of profuse apologies, and turned those beautiful and penetrating grey eyes on me, I was completely captivated. 'Don't have any delusions about it young man – you are really too old to start training, but if you work doubly hard at my school for a couple of years, I might be able to make something of you – that is if we are all still alive then!' and then she burst out laughing. This thoroughly unnerved me but I was struck by her incredible energy and honesty, which in the years to come was to make our relationship very strong. She may have sometimes been pretty difficult and occasionally angry with me, probably with good reason, but a bond of trust existed that was to become unshakeable. She was my boss until her dying day.

Madam once said that she had really wanted to be a writer. Judging by her beautiful poetry and her autobiographies, she would probably have been equally successful in this field as she was in the ballet, but luckily for us, this was not to be. What it did do, however, was to bring her understanding and appreciation of great literature into the art of choreography. Her days in Ireland working with W. B. Yeats had a profound effect on her and, as a result, most of her ballets have strong narrative themes, many of which have stood the test of time and are still being performed today. Her period as a dancer with Diaghilev also had an enormous effect on her, and she readily admitted that everything she knew about building and running a ballet company came from him. She absolutely adored the man, though she never actually managed to have a proper conversation with him. However, although she was greatly influenced by working in such close proximity to all those great composers, choreographers, painters, designers and fabulous dancers, she always insisted that it was her collaboration with Sir Frederick Ashton that had led to the style and form of the companies that she then went on to create.

Madam's association with Lilian Baylis, managing director of Sadler's Wells, is legendary, and although she gave Miss Baylis much of the credit for providing London with a permanent ballet company, a theatre, and accommodation for a school, she said that the real architects of The Royal Ballet were Frederick Ashton, Constant Lambert, Sophie Fedorovitch, Margot

Fonteyn and Robert Helpmann; and she always stressed how vitally important it had been to have Alicia Markova and Anton Dolin as leaders of the company in those early pioneering days. Typically, she just referred to herself as the housekeeper! The truth of the matter is that it was her ability to recognise and harness those great talents that made the birth of our great National Companies possible. Was it just a coincidence or was it somehow pre-ordained that at that moment in history her path should cross with all those exceptional talents? Miss Baylis, with her great faith, would have gone for the latter – 'Definitely planned by the Lord', she would have said. I tend to agree.

When John Cranko and Kenneth MacMillan showed signs of choreographic talent, she was quick to give them opportunities at Sadler's Wells, under the expert guidance of Peggy Van Praagh. She was so proud when they became internationally famous, both as choreographers and directors – John in Stuttgart and Kenneth in Berlin and then London – but their premature deaths affected her very deeply. She loved them both so much. In fact, although Madam loved her ballerinas, she was happiest when working with the men, especially when it came to her own choreography; some of her best work, particularly in *The Rake's Progress*, *Job* and *Checkmate*, was created for male dancers. Because she was very nervous, she said, about how the dancers would react to her choreography, she would put on a rather forbidding front, which often scared the living daylights out of some of her cast! The men were able to stand up to this better than the women, which of course she liked as it got her adrenaline going. Though I have to say, even the strongest of us weakened when confronted by some of her withering and devastating glances. She brought Nureyev in, she said 'To stir things up a bit'; well, it certainly did that, but it also widened *his* horizons and led to just about the most famous partnership in ballet history – Fonteyn and Nureyev – she adored them both. This really was a masterly stroke of the de Valois genius.

Oh how I wish I had seen Madam dance! Though I did once see her appear in Ashton's Wedding Bouquet as Webster, the bossy and organising maid. She was 52 and had not danced for 13 years, but it was the 21st anniversary of the company and reluctantly she had agreed to make this surprise appearance. When the curtain rose and she was revealed standing there the audience went wild – it seemed the cheers and tumultuous applause would never cease, until she raised her arm, and, with one of her commanding gestures, called for silence. I have never heard an audience switch from a deafening roar to utter silence so quickly – it was instantaneous and you could hear a pin drop. Then with a nod of her head and a twinkle in her eye, the performance began. She was witty, precise, very bold and bossy and my favourite moment was when it came to the difficult diagonal step – she took a quick look up to the gallery, wagged her finger and then marched down the diagonal with her nose in the air. This brought the house down!

Madam's vision of a National Ballet meant endless battles, which, I might say, she nearly always won, but she was plagued with ill health – Polio when she was young, arthritis, and unrelenting migraines which she rarely gave into; but her many loyal disciples in the early days, amongst them Babs Phillips, Ursula Moreton, Winifred Edwards, Joy Newton and Jill Gregory, helped her through thick and thin, as did certain very caring people who visited her regularly and looked after her affairs during the difficult last years, months and days: Pamela May, Graham Bowles, Peter Wilson, her most loyal and devoted secretary Helen Quenell, and all her wonderfully patient nurses. Although she never ceased to boss them all around, I know how deeply grateful she was for all their kindness and devotion.

During my many visits to see Dame Ninette at her home in Barnes, she often spoke of Sir John Tooley who gave her such magnificent support when he was at the helm of the Royal Opera House; she respected him enormously and always trusted his judgement. Her gratitude to Lord and Lady Sainsbury – John and Anya – who have done so much for the companies, was unbounded; and to the President of both the school and the companies, Her Royal Highness the Princess Margaret, Dame Ninette was always profoundly grateful, often saying that without her unfailing interest and help, The Royal Ballet Companies would never have reached such a prominent position in the world as that which they hold today.

My dear Madam, what you achieved in your life is unbelievable – the establishment of three major companies, The Royal Ballet, Birmingham Royal Ballet and The National Ballet of Turkey (for we must never forget that you founded and ran *that* company too, *and* its school) and then, of course, The Royal Ballet School, the bedrock of the whole organisation, which I think was really your greatest love, particularly White Lodge, where you spent your 100th birthday surrounded by the children, staff and company who were all so devoted to you. We all owe you a huge debt of gratitude for your constant supervision of the school's vocational training and for your continued presence there after your retirement, both advising and teaching. And then there are the books you wrote and your beautiful collection of poetry; your inspired speeches, unsurpassed to this day in the world of dance; lecture tours; summer schools; teachers' training courses; productions of the classics; the creation of your own ballets; world tours with that never-to-be-forgotten day when you and the company conquered New York with your production of *The Sleeping Beauty*; your support of the Royal Academy of Dance, and The Benesh Institute and countless other dance organisations. It just goes on and on and on.

During the last years of your long life of great achievement, you often said it was time for you to go but God didn't seem to want you. Well, I don't think it was really that, Madam; I think he wanted to be sure that we were ready to cope without you. I just hope we are, for you gave the world something so precious, so life enhancing, we must be sure that we never lose sight of your inspired and visionary aims.

Thank you Dame Ninette de Valois, honoured by the Queen with the Order of Merit, Companion of Honour and Dame of the British Empire, for giving thousands of us purpose, focus and fulfilment in our lives. Your words to me when I became a director: 'Respect the Past, Herald the Future, but Concentrate on the Present' will remain in my thinking forever.